# Nashua Public Library

## Enjoy this book!

Please remember to return it on time
so that others may enjoy it too.

Manage your library account and
discover all we offer by visiting us
online at www.nashualibrary.org

**Love your library? Tell a friend!**

J

AWESOME ANIMAL HEROES

# STEVE IRWIN

LAUREN KUKLA

Consulting Editor, Diane Craig, M.A./Reading Specialist

**Super Sandcastle**

An Imprint of Abdo Publishing
abdopublishing.com

# abdopublishing.com

Published by Abdo Publishing, a division of ABDO, PO Box 398166, Minneapolis, Minnesota 55439.
Copyright © 2017 by Abdo Consulting Group, Inc. International copyrights reserved in all countries.
No part of this book may be reproduced in any form without written permission from the publisher.
Super SandCastle™ is a trademark and logo of Abdo Publishing.

Printed in the United States of America, North Mankato, Minnesota
102016
012017

THIS BOOK CONTAINS
RECYCLED MATERIALS

Editor: Paige Polinsky
Content Developer: Nancy Tuminelly
Cover and Interior Design and Production: Mighty Media, Inc.
Photo Credits: AP Images, Everett Collection NYC, Shutterstock

**Publisher's Cataloging-in-Publication Data**

Names: Kukla, Lauren, author.
Title: Steve Irwin / by Lauren Kukla.
Description: Minneapolis, MN : Abdo Publishing, 2017. | Series: Awesome animal
    heroes
Identifiers: LCCN 2016944661 | ISBN 9781680784367 (lib. bdg.) |
    ISBN 9781680797893 (ebook)
Subjects:  LCSH:  Irwin, Steve, 1962-2006--Juvenile literature. | Herpetologists--
    Australia--Biography--Juvenile literature. | Naturalists--Australia--Biography-
    -Juvenile literature. | Wildlife conservation--Australia--Biography--Juvenile
    literature.
Classification: DDC 597.9092 [B]--dc23
LC record available at http://lccn.loc.gov/2016944661

Super SandCastle™ books are created by a team of professional educators, reading specialists, and content developers around five essential components—phonemic awareness, phonics, vocabulary, text comprehension, and fluency—to assist young readers as they develop reading skills and strategies and increase their general knowledge. All books are written, reviewed, and leveled for guided reading, early reading intervention, and Accelerated Reader™ programs for use in shared, guided, and independent reading and writing activities to support a balanced approach to literacy instruction.

# CONTENTS

# THE CROCODILE HUNTER

Steve Irwin was a **conservationist**. He worked to protect wildlife. He is best known for his work with crocodiles. He was even known as the Crocodile Hunter! But Irwin actually tried to prevent crocodile hunting. He caught crocs that were in danger.

*Steve Irwin*

# STEVE IRWIN

**BORN:** February 22, 1962, Melbourne, Victoria, Australia

**MARRIED:** Terri Raines Irwin, June 4, 1992

**CHILDREN:** Bindi Irwin, Robert Irwin

**DIED:** September 4, 2006

# EARLY LIFE

Steve was born Stephen Robert Irwin. His parents were Bob and Lyn. Steve grew up in Beerwah, Australia. His parents ran a wildlife park there. The park was home to kangaroos and crocodiles. Snakes and other animals also lived there.

*Beerwah is in the state of Queensland, Australia.*

# A LOVE OF REPTILES

Irwin's family loved animals. Bob was a **herpetologist**. Lyn cared for hurt animals. Young Steve and his two sisters worked at the park. Steve loved reptiles the most. He helped his father catch crocodiles.

The Irwin's park was called the Beerwah Reptile and Fauna Park. It was later renamed the Australia Zoo.

# STARTING WORK

After high school, Irwin worked at his family's park. He also worked for the Australian government. Irwin trapped problem crocodiles. Some of them lived too close to people. Others were in danger from **poachers**. Irwin sometimes videotaped his work. A television producer saw the tapes. He wanted Irwin to make a TV movie!

Irwin's dog Sui often went with him on his croc-catching trips.

# TV AND FAMILY

Irwin's movie aired in 1992. It was called *The Crocodile Hunter*. Meanwhile, Irwin was running the wildlife park. He married Terri Raines on June 4, 1992. They had two children. Bindi was born in 1998. Robert was born in 2003.

*Terri, Robert, and Bindi Irwin*

# CRIKEY!

Viewers loved Irwin's movie. So it became a series. On the show, Irwin caught crocodiles and other animals. Irwin only caught animals that were in danger. He moved them to safer areas. He warned about ruining animal **habitats**. By 1996, *The Crocodile Hunter* was shown around the world.

*Irwin worked with many different animals on his TV show, including snakes.*

# CATCHING CROCS

Steve and Terri worked together to catch crocodiles. Sometimes they set traps with nets. Irwin also **wrestled** crocs. First he jumped on the animal's back. Then he tied the croc's jaws shut. He covered the croc's eyes. This kept it calm. Then Irwin could safely move the animal.

*Crocodiles live near rivers and along coastlines.*

*Irwin's methods for safely catching and moving crocodiles are still used.*

# WILDLIFE WARRIORS

Irwin cared about all animals. He and Terri started Wildlife Warriors in 2002. It works to protect animals and their **habitats**.

*Bindi is very active in Wildlife Warriors.*

In 2004, Wildlife Warriors opened an animal hospital. It is at the Australia Zoo in Queensland, Australia.

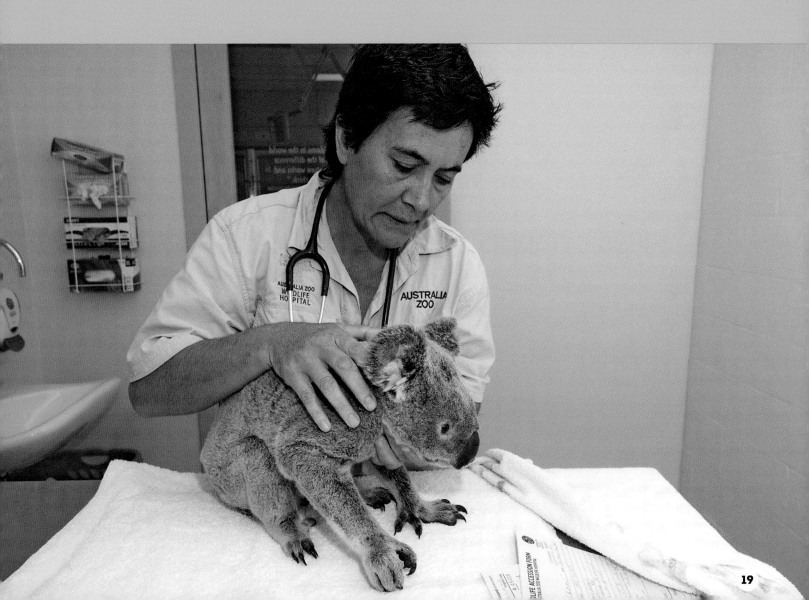

# A LIFE'S WORK

Irwin spent his life fighting for animals. In 2006, he was filming **stingrays** near Australia. A stingray stabbed Irwin. He died shortly after. But his family carries on his work. Irwin changed the way people see crocodiles and other wildlife.

*Stingrays protect themselves with sharp, poisonous tails.*

(above) *Bindi Irwin in 2006*

(left) *Steve Irwin*

# MORE ABOUT IRWIN

Steve Irwin first worked with CROCODILES when he was nine years old.

Australians celebrate STEVE IRWIN DAY each November 15. They honor Irwin's life and work.

*Crocodile Hunter* was shown in more than 100 COUNTRIES.

# TEST YOUR KNOWLEDGE

1. In what country was Irwin born?

2. When did Irwin start Wildlife Warriors?

3. Irwin was killed by a crocodile. True or false?

## THINK ABOUT IT!

What is your favorite reptile? Why do you like it?

**ANSWERS:** 1. Australia 2. 2002 3. False

# GLOSSARY

**conservationist** – a person who saves or protects something.

**habitat** – the area or environment where a person or animal usually lives.

**herpetologist** – a scientist who studies reptiles and amphibians, such as crocodiles and frogs.

**poacher** – someone who hunts or fishes illegally.

**stingray** – a type of fish that has a large, flat body and a long tail with spines on it that are used to sting other animals.

**wrestle** – to fight by grabbing, pushing, and pulling instead of hitting, kicking, or punching.